Dates of a Decade

THE 1950s

Paul Harrison

W
FRANKLIN WATTS
LONDON•SYDNEY

First printed in paperback in 2013

First published in 2008 by Franklin Watts
Reprinted 2009

© 2008 Arcturus Publishing Limited

Franklin Watts
338 Euston Road
London NW1 3BH

Franklin Watts Australia
Level 17/207 Kent Street, Sydney, NSW 2000

Produced by Arcturus Publishing Limited,
26/27 Bickels Yard, 151–153 Bermondsey Street,
London SE1 3HA

The right of Paul Harrison to be identified as the author
of this work has been asserted by him in accordance
with the Copyright, Designs and Patents Act 1988.

Series concept: Alex Woolf
Editor and picture researcher: Alex Woolf
Designer: Phipps Design

Picture credits:
Corbis: cover (top) (Condé Nast Archive), 4 (Bettmann), 5 (Bettmann), 6 (Bettmann),
7 (Bettmann), 8 (Hulton-Deutsch Collection), 9 (Hulton-Deutsch Collection),
12 (Bettmann), 13 (Dmitri Baltermants/ The Dmitri Baltermants Collection),
15 (Reuters), 16 (Bettmann), 18 (Bettmann), 19 (Owen Franken), 20 (Bettmann),
21 (Sandy Felsenthal), 22 (Sunset Boulevard), 23 (John Springer Collection),
24 (Bettmann), 26 (Hulton-Deutsch Collection), 27 (Hulton-Deutsch Collection),
28 (Hulton-Deutsch Collection), 29 (Hulton-Deutsch Collection), cover (right) and
31 (Bettmann), 33 (Bettmann), 34 (Rykoff Collection), 35 (Bettmann),
36 (Bettmann), cover (bottom) and 37 (Granma/Stringer/Reuters), 38 (Frédéric
Neema/Sygma), 39 (Bettmann), 40 (Hulton-Deutsch Collection), 41 (Hulton-Deutsch
Collection), 42 (Hulton-Deutsch Collection), 43 (Hulton-Deutsch Collection),
44 (Klaus Heirler/dpa), 45 (Hulton-Deutsch Collection).
Science Photo Library: 11 (A Barrington Brown).
Shutterstock: 14 (Jose Fuente).

Every attempt has been made to clear copyright. Should there be any inadvertent
omission, please apply to the publisher for rectification.

A CIP catalogue record for this book is available from the British Library.

Dewey Decimal Classification Number: 909.82' 5

ISBN 978 1 4451 1879 6

Printed in China

Franklin Watts is a division of Hachette Children's Books,
an Hachette UK Company
www.hachette.co.uk

Supplier 03, Date 0213, Print Run 2354
SL000835EN

Contents

GLOBAL EVENTS

BRITISH EVENTS

The McCarthy Witch Hunts

Soon after the end of World War II (1939–1945), tensions began to rise between the USA and the communist Soviet Union, and their respective allies. Each side believed the other was trying to overthrow its government and replace it with a government that supported its own, opposing ideology. This conflict was known as the Cold War, as no direct military engagements took place between the main opponents, although the threat of an all-out nuclear conflict was always there.

In February 1950, at the height of Cold War anxiety, an American politician from the Republican Party, Senator Joseph McCarthy, stood up to make a speech in Wheeling, West Virginia, and tapped right into the nightmares of the American people – he claimed that the US government itself had been infiltrated by communist spies.

Joseph McCarthy is seen here in typically belligerent style during an appearance at a Senate investigation into communist infiltration in the State Department in March 1950.

'Communists in the government'

In his speech, McCarthy began by painting a grim picture of how the USA was outnumbered by the communist powers to the east. Then he made a dramatic claim: 'I have here in my hand a list of 205 … a list of names that were made known to the Secretary of State as being members of the Communist Party and who nevertheless are still working and shaping policy in the State Department.'

The papers ran the story and public fears were whipped up, especially as McCarthy continued to make his allegations despite never providing substantial proof. Eleven days later, Senator McCarthy gave a six-hour speech to Congress where he identified over 80 people – though not by name – who he claimed were communist sympathizers. Again he supplied little proof, but despite this the story struck a chord and won popular support.

Interrogating suspects

Partly as a result of McCarthy's actions, the Republicans won the presidential elections in 1952. Afterwards, McCarthy was made chairman of the Committee on Government Operations and began to interrogate suspected communists in many areas of American life. Politicians and academics were hounded from office; journalists, writers, film-makers and actors were blacklisted (shunned by their profession), and people from all walks of life were persecuted if they were even suspected of having left-wing views. Colleague testified against colleague at special hearings set up to root out communist sympathizers.

However McCarthy's reign of terror lasted only until 1954. He met his match when trying to get an army officer, Captain Irving Peress, court-martialled for alleged 'un-American' attitudes. McCarthy failed, and the US public, tired of seeing America fighting with itself, turned against the senator. He was relieved of his position soon afterwards.

McCarthy was always big news. Here he is surrounded by journalists in a lunch break during a hearing in September 1954.

What the papers said

Senator Joseph R McCarthy ... asserted that spies had been planted in the State Department to shape the policy of our government and rob this nation of its potency.... Sen. McCarthy brought gasps from some members of his audience and there were tears in the eyes of others as he made his case.

The Reno Evening Gazette, 13 February 1950

- **SEE ALSO**
  Pages 6–7: 25 June 1950:
  The Korean War Begins

- **FURTHER INFORMATION**
- 📖 Books:
  Snapshots in History: McCarthyism: The Red Scare by Brian Fitzgerald (Compass Point, 2006)
- 🕮 Websites:
  historymatters.gmu.edu/d/6456
  McCarthy's Wheeling speech

25
JUNE
1950

The Korean War Begins

By the end of World War II the country of Korea was split in two along a line known as the 38th parallel. The Soviet army occupied the north and the Americans the south. Originally, elections had been planned to unite the country, but in the climate of mistrust that existed between the USA and the Soviet Union, these polls never took place and the country remained divided. In 1948, governments were set up in each country. The communists took control of the north under the rule of Kim Il Sung, while in the south, Syngman Rhee and his anti-communist government were elected to power.

General MacArthur (in the black jacket) inspects facilities at Inchon on 16 September 1950, the day after UN forces landed there.

Invasion

In 1950, with the new South Korean government established, the American troops left. Then, during the early hours of 25 June, North Korea invaded the South in an attempt to reunite Korea by force. The North Korean advance was rapid and the army quickly overran the South Korean capital of Seoul. At this stage it appeared that the North would completely occupy the South.

The Americans, already concerned at the prospect of communist expansion in South-East Asia, were swift to respond. Troops were immediately dispatched and assistance was sought from the United Nations (UN) on the grounds that a democratically elected government was being overthrown by force. The UN agreed to help and the American forces were joined by troops sent from Britain, Australia and other Western countries. The UN forces, under the command of US general Douglas MacArthur, landed at a place called Inchon, in occupied territory, on 15 September 1950, and proceeded to force back the North Koreans beyond the 38th parallel.

Counterattack

The goal of liberating South Korea had been achieved. But the easy victory encouraged the Americans – with UN approval – to continue the fight with the aim of reuniting Korea under the government of Syngman Rhee. The UN forces took the North Korean capital, Pyongyang, on 19 October 1950.

However, just as it looked as if the UN forces would completely occupy North Korea, China came to the aid of its communist neighbour. Together, China and North Korea mounted a counter-offensive that forced the UN forces into retreat, and Seoul fell once more on 4 January 1951.

The UN forces rallied and advanced northwards again, until a stalemate was reached in the autumn of 1951. Eventually a ceasefire was agreed at midnight on 27 July 1953 and the border was set near the 38th parallel, where it had been originally. The two countries are still technically at war today and an uneasy ceasefire remains.

A wounded American soldier is carried to safety by his comrades during a battle in July 1953.

- **SEE ALSO**
  Pages 4–5: 9 February 1950:
  The McCarthy Witch Hunts

- **FURTHER INFORMATION**
- 📖 Books:
  North and South Korea
  by Cath Senker (Wayland, 2011)
- Websites:
  www.historycentral.com/korea/index.html
  Major events of the Korean War

What the papers said

The outbreak of hostilities in Korea is particularly serious in the world's eyes because the two contending armies are so akin to their foster parents, the Soviet Union and the United States.

The New York Times, 26 June 1950

The First Commercial Jet Airliner

When passengers at London's Heathrow Airport boarded the British Overseas Aircraft Corporation's plane, G-ALYP, they were more than usually excited. Air travel was still the preserve of the wealthy, but this history-making flight was about to change all that; this was the maiden flight of the de Havilland Comet, the world's first commercial jet airliner.

A new era

Jet-powered aircraft were first developed during World War II, but until 1952 had been used for fighter aircraft, not passenger planes. Commercial air travel had relied on propeller-driven planes that were slow, noisy and expensive. The Comet's sleek, modern lines heralded a new era of speed and comfort. The plane was capable of carrying up to 44 passengers, which was actually fewer than some of its propeller-driven rivals, but it had a top speed of almost 800 kilometres per hour, which was nearly twice as fast as most of the competition.

The first passengers board the BOAC Comet for its maiden flight from London Heathrow to Johannesburg.

The sleek lines of the Comet, combined with its revolutionary jet engines, heralded the future of commercial air travel.

This cutting-edge technology was beyond the means of most people. The Comet was initially used for the prestigious London-to-Johannesburg route, and its passengers all tended to be very wealthy. Today, an aeroplane could travel this distance directly, but the Comet required refuelling stops at Rome, Beirut, Khartoum, Entebbe and Livingstone. The whole journey took around 23 hours.

Design flaw

Disaster was to strike the Comet though. A serious design flaw caused the cabin walls to give way around the windows. This resulted in a number of fatal crashes in 1953 and 1954, and the entire fleet of planes was grounded in 1954. The Comet flew again in 1958 but was forever tainted by the tragedies that had befallen it earlier that decade.

In its brief career, however, the Comet did point the way forwards for air travel. Other manufacturers were quick to see the advantages of commercial jet airliners, and as faster and bigger planes were built, ticket prices dropped. The Comet that took off that January morning in 1952 represented the first step on the road to mass air travel.

eye witness

There's no real impression of speed while you are in the air, it's only when you flash by an occasional cloud that there's any real impression of movement. For most of the time it's like being suspended in space, with the clouds far below and the sky in daytime a deeper blue because of the height. It's quieter than the normal passenger aeroplane and it's quite easy to carry on a conversation.

Douglas Willis, a passenger on the maiden flight.
Quoted from news.bbc.co.uk/onthisday/hi/dates/stories/may/2/newsid_2480000/2480339.stm

- **SEE ALSO**
  Pages 34–35: 4 October 1957:
  Sputnik is Launched

- **FURTHER INFORMATION**
  Books:
  High Times: A History of Aviation
  by Golden Cosmos (Nobrow Ltd, 2012)
  Websites:
  www.rafmuseum.org.uk/research/archive-exhibitions/comet-the-worlds-first-jet-airliner.aspx
  All about the Comet

DNA is Discovered

It was a damp February day when the young scientists Francis Crick and James Watson walked into the Eagle public house in Cambridge, UK, for some lunch. They often ate there after working in their nearby laboratory. However, today was no ordinary day. They had made a discovery that morning that would revolutionize the world of science and medicine. 'We have found the secret of life,' announced Crick as they entered the pub. He was not far wrong.

The code of life

What Crick and Watson had found was the structure of a macromolecule (a tiny amount of a chemical substance) called deoxyribonucleic acid – or DNA. DNA is important because it contains the genetic code for life. In other words, it determines how a living thing will grow and what it will look like. For example, it is through our DNA that we inherit characteristics from our parents, be it the colour of our hair or the height we will reach. DNA is what makes oak trees look like oak trees or ladybirds like ladybirds.

Scientists had known what DNA did and were pretty sure of what it was made of, but importantly they had no idea of how it was made or what it looked like. This is what Crick and Watson set out to discover. Instead of conducting experiments like other scientists, they spent time imagining what they thought it *should* look like. They thought it would probably be a double helix with molecules in between – essentially they believed it would look something like a twisted ladder. What they needed now was proof.

Nobel Prize

Their breakthrough came when they were shown an image from a special kind of X-ray, which supported their idea. Crick and Watson published

⊙ **eye** witness

We wish to suggest a structure for the salt of deoxyribose nucleic acid (DNA). This structure has novel features which are of considerable biological interest…. A structure for nucleic acid has already been proposed by Pauling and Corey. They kindly made their manuscript available to us in advance of publication. Their model consists of three intertwined chains, with the phosphates near the fibre axis, and the bases on the outside. In our opinion, this structure is unsatisfactory…. We wish to put forward a radically different structure for the salt of deoxyribose nucleic acid. This structure has two helical chains each coiled around the same axis….

Quoted from the letter Crick and Watson published in *Nature*, 25 April 1953 their findings in *Nature* magazine, but not many people understood the significance of the breakthrough at first. As other scientists found evidence that corroborated Crick and Watson's theory, interest gradually grew. The pair were eventually awarded a Nobel Prize in 1962 for their discovery.

There was some controversy over the award. The X-ray image they had seen belonged to a scientist called Rosalind Franklin. She was close to discovering the structure of DNA herself, and had not given permission for Crick and Watson to see the image. She died aged 37 in 1958 without being given the credit that she deserved for her part in the discovery.

James Watson (left) and Francis Crick inspect their model of the structure of DNA at their laboratory in Cambridge.

- **SEE ALSO**
  Pages 18–19: 23 December 1954:
  The First Organ Transplant

- **FURTHER INFORMATION**
- Books:
  Watson and Crick and Their Discovery of DNA
  by Anne Rooney
  (Evans Brothers Ltd, 2013)
- Websites:
  library.thinkquest.org/20830/Textbook/
  HistoryofDNAResearch.htm
  A brief history of DNA research

Stalin Dies

After four days in a coma following a massive stroke, Joseph Stalin, General Secretary of the Communist Party and leader of the Soviet Union, died. He had controlled the communist world with an iron fist for a quarter of a century and was feared equally at home and abroad. His death appeared to promise a new era for the entire world.

Rise to power

It had been quite a journey for Stalin. He was a Georgian, not a Russian, born in 1879 and christened Josef Vissarionovich Dzhugashvili. He had an unconventional upbringing. As a child, he suffered beatings by his father and was later expelled from a seminary (a training school for priests) for studying the works of Karl Marx. He became a revolutionary with the communist Bolshevik party and edited their paper, *Pravda*.

In October 1917, a revolution brought the communists to power in Russia. In 1922, all the states that had been under Russian control joined with Russia to form the Union of Soviet Socialist Republics (USSR), or the Soviet Union. Stalin was appointed General Secretary of the Communist Party. Two years later, the Soviet leader, Vladimir Lenin, died. Stalin used his position to create a strong power base within the party and to defeat his rivals, enabling him to become absolute ruler of the Soviet Union by 1928.

This official portrait of Joseph Stalin dates from around 1940.

How it was reported

The Central Committee ... announce with deep grief to the party and all workers that on March 5 at 9.50 pm, Josef Vissarionovich Stalin died after a serious illness. The heart of the collaborator and follower of the genius of Lenin's work, the wise leader and teacher of the Communist party and of the Soviet people, stopped beating.

Moscow Home Service, 7 March 1953

Stalin's rule

Stalin led the Soviet Union with a mixture of charisma and fear. He could be an inspirational leader, and turned a primarily agricultural nation into an industrial superpower. But this came at a terrible cost: conditions both in the cities and in the countryside were grim, and many people starved. During the 1930s, Stalin executed millions of people and imprisoned millions more in slave labour camps, claiming they were enemies of the state. He displayed a similar indifference to people's lives during World War II. Although his Red Army eventually defeated the invading Germans, the Soviet Union suffered more casualties than every other combatant nation combined, partly due to the tactics Stalin encouraged.

After the war, Stalin succumbed to increasing paranoia, and the arrests and imprisonments continued until his death. Many Soviet citizens mourned Stalin's passing, despite his monstrous deeds. They believed in his ideals and were proud that he had made the Soviet Union a great world power. However, a large number of people were secretly relieved. It is estimated that under Stalin's leadership, around 20 million Soviet citizens were executed, 18 million were sent to slave labour camps, and a further 10 million were deported. Three years after his death, Stalin's successor, Nikita Khrushchev, made a speech denouncing what Stalin had done.

Soviet factory workers gather around a radio to hear the announcement of Stalin's death.

- **SEE ALSO**
Pages 28–29: 4 November 1956: The Hungarian Uprising is Crushed

- **FURTHER INFORMATION**
  - Books:
  Joseph Stalin by Sean McCollum (Franklin Watts, 2010)
  - Websites:
  www.spartacus.schoolnet.co.uk/RUSstalin.htm Biography of Stalin

Everest is Conquered

As Edmund Hillary and Tenzing Norgay ate breakfast by their tents on a clear dawn near the top of Mount Everest, they knew the day would end either in triumph or intense disappointment. Months of planning and weeks of trekking lay behind them. Further down the mountain was the rest of the expedition that John Hunt had organized to make an attempt on the summit. Ahead of them in the snow were the footprints of the team that had tried and failed to reach the summit just three days earlier. If Hillary and Tenzing also failed, the team would most likely have to return home as the bad monsoon weather was closing in. This was their last chance.

The roof of the world

Mount Everest is the highest mountain in the world. It sits among the Himalayan mountain range in Nepal and rises 8,849 metres. Its height was first calculated by surveyors working for Britain in 1854. The surveyors called the mountain Peak XV. It was later named after the man who organized the survey, Sir George Everest. The Nepalese themselves call the mountain Chomolungma. Whatever its name, the mountain is a dangerous

Mount Everest, the highest mountain in the world. Hillary and Tenzing approached the summit from the left of the peak.

14

place of avalanches, high winds, severe storms and, in its upper areas, little oxygen. It had never been climbed. Many had tried but all had failed, and some did not live to tell the tale.

The expedition leader, John Hunt, was meticulous in his preparations. He assembled a large team of 13 climbers and doctors, as well as a team of Sherpas – local people who lived near the foot of Everest – who helped carry the equipment. Hunt's team also used the most up-to-date technology, including oxygen cylinders to help the climbers breathe at high altitudes. Now, 102 days after leaving Britain, the success or failure of the expedition had come down to the abilities of two climbers – and luck.

Reaching the summit

For Hillary and Tenzing, the final stage of the climb was gruelling. It was made more difficult by a 17-metre-high lump of rock and snow that had to be squirmed up like a chimney – all this while carrying oxygen tanks and swathed in multiple layers of clothing. Finally, at 11.30 am, Hillary and Tenzing made it – they had reached the highest point on earth.

They spent only 15 minutes on the summit as they needed to return to camp before their oxygen ran out. There were no satellite phones in the 1950s, so it was days before the news of their triumph reached the outside world.

Tenzing Norgay (left) and Edmund Hillary relax at their camp at Thyangboche, Nepal, following their successful climb to the summit of Everest.

eye witness

Far from failure, this was IT! They had made it!! Feelings welled up uncontrollably as I now quickened my pace…. The next moment I was with them: handshakes – even I blush to say, hugs – for the triumphant pair. A special one for Tenzing, so well merited for him personally, this victory, both for himself and for his people.

John Hunt in his book *The Ascent of Everest* (London Readers Union, 1955)

- **SEE ALSO**
  Pages 16–17: 6 May 1954:
  Breaking the Four-Minute Mile

- **FURTHER INFORMATION**
  Books:
  Conquering Mount Everest by Robert Sheehan (PowerKids Press, 2013)
  Websites:
  imagingeverest.rgs.org/Concepts/Virtual_Everest/-75.html
  For information on Everest and all the Everest expeditions, from the Royal Geographical Society

Breaking the Four-Minute Mile

It was a blustery day at the cinder race track at Iffley Road in Oxford, UK. The event was the annual competition between Oxford University and the Amateur Athletics Association (AAA). However, this year was to be a little bit special. Roger Bannister, a 25-year-old runner from the AAA and former student of Oxford University, was trying to accomplish one of the greatest feats in athletics history – he was going to try to run a mile in under four minutes.

Careful preparation

Although a number of runners had come close to breaking the four-minute barrier, no one had yet managed it. This led many people to believe that it was physically impossible. Bannister had other ideas. He knew that preparation was key. To help him, he arranged for there to be two pacemakers – athletes who would set the pace for Bannister by running for

An exhausted Roger Bannister crosses the finish line after his successful attempt at one of the most prized records in world athletics.

as long as possible at record-breaking pace. He would run behind them, then take over for the last section of the race as the pacemakers tired. The pacemakers were Chris Brasher and Chris Chataway.

On the day of the competition it was quite gusty – hardly ideal conditions for a record-breaking run – and the attempt was very nearly called off. However, the wind dropped slightly as the race was about to begin, and Bannister decided to try for the record. A false start added to the already tense atmosphere. The athletes were pulled back for a restart, much to Bannister's annoyance as he was worried that the wind would pick up again.

The miracle mile

When the race finally got underway, the first pacemaker, Chris Brasher, maintained the perfect pace to break the record. The first half mile was completed in 1 minute 58 seconds and shortly afterwards the second pacemaker, Chris Chataway, moved past Bannister and Brasher to take up the lead. He too did a brilliant job. Around 200 metres from the finish line, Bannister himself moved into the lead. This was the best chance anyone had had to break the record and Bannister was not about to throw it away. To the roars of the 3,000 spectators, he found a final burst of energy and crossed the line in a time of 3 minutes 59.4 seconds – immediately collapsing into the arms of a friend.

Bannister's magnificent achievement is regarded as one of the greatest moments in athletics history. His record was broken the very next month by the Australian runner John Landy, and Bannister himself retired from racing by the end of the year to pursue his medical studies. But he had cemented his place in history as the man who ran the 'miracle mile'.

◉ eye witness

It was the most memorable race I ever ran and I remember all the details. I knew the record attempt was on because Bannister asked me to keep out of his way on the first two laps.... It was an exhilarating night and I was proud to have taken part in such a historic race.

Tom Hulatt, who came third in the race. Quoted in www.tommyhulatt.org.uk/

What the papers said

The dream of world athletes through the years was achieved yesterday by an Englishman – 25-year-old Roger Bannister, who became the first man on earth to run a mile in under four minutes. His feat at Oxford last evening – against a 20-mile-an-hour cross-wind was equal in dramatic achievement to the crashing of the sound barrier in the air.

Daily Express, 7 May 1954

• **SEE ALSO**
Pages 14–15: 29 May 1953:
Everest is Conquered

• **FURTHER INFORMATION**
📖 Books:
The First Four Minutes by Roger Bannister
(Sutton Publishing, 2004)
Websites:
www.guardian.co.uk/sport/2004/may/01/athletics
Roger Bannister recalls the race

The First Organ Transplant

It was two days before Christmas when 23-year-old Ronald Herrick gave his twin brother Richard an early and most unusual present. For Richard, who was dying of a kidney disease, it was probably the best present he could have received. Ronald donated one of his own kidneys in order to give his brother the best chance of survival. Now Richard had to undergo a very risky surgical procedure: the transplant of a major organ.

Overcoming rejection

Organ transplants had been tried before but had never worked. The body of the transplant recipient always rejected the new organ. The body's immune system (defence mechanism) regarded the new organ as something foreign to itself and therefore harmful, and attacked it. Doctors needed to find some way of convincing the immune system that the new organ was not foreign.

Joseph Murray, the surgeon who was to perform the operation, had good reason to believe that this time things would be different. Richard and Ronald were identical twins – they had come from the same egg – so biologically they were very similar. Consequently, the immune system might not recognize the new kidney as being foreign.

However, there was an ethical issue that had to be addressed before the operation could be performed. By taking a kidney from Ronald, the surgical team could be seen as contravening a doctor's duty not to cause harm to a patient. Some people were not even sure a person could live with one kidney. The members of the surgical team were convinced, however, that Ronald would be fine and that the operation was ethical.

Richard Herrick (seated) is pushed from the Peter Bent Brigham hospital in Boston, Massachusetts, USA, by his twin brother Ronald following their successful kidney transplant.

eye witness

We didn't think we made history, we didn't even think of history. We thought we were going to save a patient.

Joseph Murray, quoted in www.npr.org/templates/story/story.php?storyId=4233669

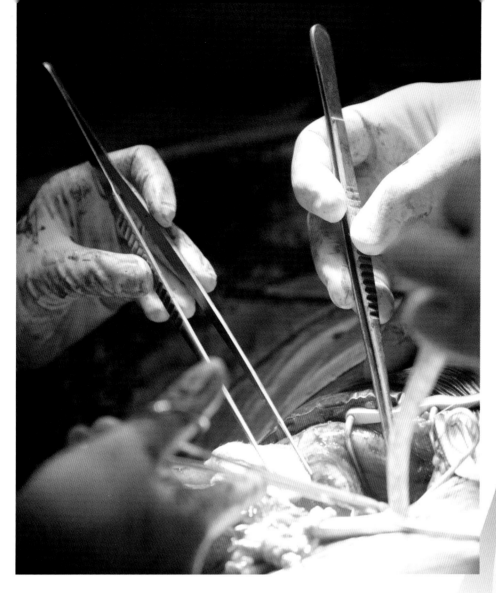

Surgeons at work during a modern kidney transplant operation.

The operation

Murray knew he had just one chance at the operation – after all, Ronald had only one spare kidney – so Murray organized a trial run using a dead body. He wanted to be sure that he knew exactly what he was doing when the real operation began.

The real operation started at 8.15 am and lasted for over three hours. First, the healthy kidney had to be removed from Ronald. When this was done, the more difficult procedure of attaching it to Richard was carried out. Fortunately everything went smoothly, much to the relief of all concerned.

Richard Herrick's body did not reject the kidney, but he lived only another eight years. Nevertheless, the operation was a great success for its time, and paved the way for more successful organ transplants in the future. Ronald Herrick lived into his 70s.

- **SEE ALSO**
Pages 10–11: 28 February 1953:
DNA is discovered

- **FURTHER INFORMATION**
📖 Books:
Organ Transplants
by Melissa Abramovitz (Lucent Books, 2012)
🖱 Websites:
www.donatelifeny.org/all-about-transplantation/
organ-transplant-history
Click on the link on the page to read an interview
with Joseph Murray

The First McDonald's Franchise Opens

Ray Kroc had always had an eye for a business opportunity. The problem was that a real opportunity had never come his way before. During the early 1950s he worked as a salesman, marketing milkshake mixers across the USA. He was on a routine visit to one of his customers in California when Kroc saw his chance. His customers were two brothers who owned and ran a hamburger and milkshake restaurant. The business was doing so well they were running eight of Kroc's milkshake mixers all day long. The restaurant was called McDonald's.

Ray Kroc, the man who turned McDonald's from a single fast-food restaurant into a global phenomenon.

A winning formula

What made the McDonald brothers' operation stand out was its simplicity. Their restaurant had no tables and chairs and the cutlery was made of plastic. The menu was limited, offering around nine different items, and it was cheap: a hamburger cost only 15 cents (around five pence). However, the biggest selling point of the business was that it was quick: a hamburger took under a minute to prepare and hand over to the customer. The restaurant offered fast food for people in a hurry.

Ray Kroc could envisage thousands of McDonald's restaurants right across the country. He tried to sell the idea to the brothers, Dick and Mac, but they weren't convinced. They had already sold some franchises – the right of other businesses to use their name – and hadn't made any money. Besides, they didn't have the time or energy to run a major franchising operation. Kroc, however, did. He offered to set up the franchises and pay the brothers a small share of the profits. They agreed, and in April 1955 Kroc opened the first of the new McDonald's franchises in Des Plaines, Illinois.

◉ eye witness

A chocolate malt. I had two hamburgers and french fries. And hamburgers were 15 cents a piece? Something like that, right. I think it was 53 cents for the whole meal.

Glen Volkman, one of the first McDonald's customers. Quoted in abclocal.go.com/wls/story?section=News&id=2973642

The original McDonald's in Des Plaines no longer exists, but a replica has been built further down the street and houses the McDonald's Museum.

Kroc's master stroke

Kroc stayed true to the McDonald brothers' methods. He kept the same limited menu and cheap prices. The Des Plaines business was a success, and by the end of 1956 there were 13 other McDonald's around the country. Kroc's master stroke was to make all of the restaurants identical. They would serve the same food cooked in the same way for the same price and they would all be clean – Kroc was rightly obsessed with the idea that people like clean restaurants.

It was a winning formula. By the end of the decade there were over 200 McDonald's across the mid-west and western USA. By 1970 there were over 1,500, including 50 in Canada. Kroc was a wealthy man. The McDonald brothers were also rich, though not as rich as they might have been. Kroc, ever the businessman, had persuaded the brothers to sell him their rights in the business for $2.7 million (around £1 million) in 1963. In 1965, Kroc's stake in the business was worth $32 million (around £11.5 million). And the company kept on growing. In 2012, there were over 33,000 McDonald's restaurants in about 120 countries around the world.

⊙ eye witness

I grew up in Des Plaines. I was only 6 years old in 1955 but a bit later I remember some adults giving their opinion that it is 'just a passing fad'. So much for that thought! Later, when I was in college, during a couple of summers, I was a substitute mail carrier for the Post Office. Often, I would get the route that included this restaurant (at the time it was still an operating restaurant) and I would stop in to have a Coke or if at lunch time, probably something to eat.

Unknown McDonald's customer. Quoted on www.waymarking.com/wm/details.aspx?f=1&guid =7a495d16-e89e-48f6-ae99-18420986253d&gid=4

- **SEE ALSO**
  Pages 38–39: 9 March 1959:
  Barbie is Launched

- **FURTHER INFORMATION**
  📖 Books:
  The Story of McDonald's
  by Sara Gilbert (Creative Paperbacks, 2011)
  Websites:
  www.mcdonalds.com/us/en/our_story/our_history.html
  The official history of McDonald's

30
SEPTEMBER
1955

James Dean Dies

James Dean seemingly had it all. He was young, good-looking and was experiencing a meteoric rise to fame. He had just finished shooting his latest film, *Giant*, and was now off to take part in the other love of his life, motor racing. He and his mechanic were heading to Salinas in California, where Dean was due to race. They would never get there. An oncoming car turned into the path of Dean's Porsche Spyder. The driver was apparently unable to see the silver sports car in the twilight. The two cars met head on and Dean's Porsche was sent hurtling into a ditch. Dean was dead before the ambulance could get him to hospital.

Rising star

James Byron Dean was born on 8 February 1931 in Marion, Indiana, USA. When he was 19, he studied acting at the James Whitmore acting workshop, and went on to study drama at the University of California, Los Angeles. He left his university course part way through in 1951 to pursue his acting career. Dean appeared in a number of television shows and theatre productions, but only made three major motion pictures. These were all filmed over a period of about 12 months in 1954 and 1955 and catapulted Dean into the major league of film stars.

James Dean in his iconic sports jacket and white tee-shirt.

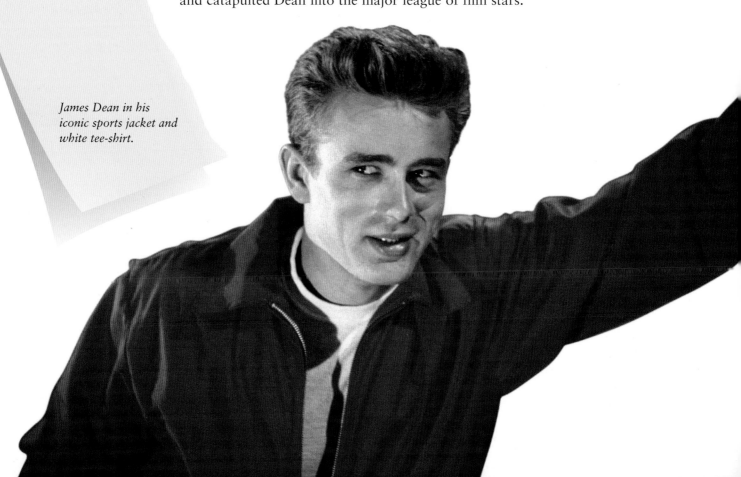

The first film he appeared in was *East of Eden*. This was directed by Elia Kazan, one of the main informants during the McCarthy witch-hunts. However, Dean really made his mark in the films *Rebel without a Cause* and *Giant*. Dean would never know the enormous impact he would make with these films as they were released after his death.

A love of speed

Dean seemed to epitomize the 'live fast, die young' mentality, with his dynamic and unpredictable acting style and his part-time motor-racing career. He raced three times and acquitted himself well, finishing second in one of the races. It was often suspected that Dean's love of speed contributed to his accident. But although it was true that he had been stopped for speeding earlier on that fateful night, analysis of the crash site carried out in 2005 suggests that Dean's car had been travelling below the speed limit at the time of the accident.

The fact that Dean died young, just as his career was taking off, undoubtedly contributed to his fame. He would never grow old, or star in bad films, and he would always be the good-looking, edgy actor who died too soon. Dean's legacy was immediate. He became the first actor to be nominated for an Academy Award after he had died. In fact he received not one but two posthumous nominations, for his roles in *East of Eden* and *Giant*.

The mangled remains of Dean's Porsche Spyder lie by the side of the road at the scene of the accident. Remarkably Dean's passenger, Rolf Wutherich, survived the crash.

What the papers said

James Dean, 24, one of Hollywood's brightest new motion-picture stars, was killed early last night in a head-on collision at the rural town of Cholame, about 19 miles east of Paso Robles.... The young actor met death in his German-built Porsche sports car while en route to road races at Salinas.... Under contract to Warner Brothers studios, the intense young star frequently had been compared to Marlon Brando and both were products of director Elia Kazan's school for tyro actors.

Los Angeles Times, 1 October 1955

• **SEE ALSO**
Pages 30–31: 6 January 1957:
Elvis is Censored

• **FURTHER INFORMATION**

📖 Books:
American Rebels: James Dean: Dream as If You'll Live Forever by Karen Clemens Warrick (Enslow Publishers, 2006)

🖱 Websites:
www.jamesdean.com/
The official James Dean website

01
DECEMBER
1955

Rosa Parks Refuses to Move Seats

By the 1950s, slavery had been abolished in the USA for almost 100 years. Despite this, African Americans continued to suffer discrimination in the southern states. In the town of Montgomery, Alabama, for example, black Americans were not allowed to mix with whites in many public places, including public transport. On Montgomery's buses black Americans had to sit in the back half of the bus – and even then, if the front half was full, they were expected to give up their seats for white Americans. As no black person was allowed to sit in the same row as a white person, up to four black people were often forced to give up their seats for the sake of a single white person.

Arrest and trial

On the evening of 1 December 1955, Rosa Parks, a 42-year-old black American, was returning from work in Montgomery. The bus was full and she and the other people in her row were asked to move so a white person could sit down. After some grumbling, three people got up, but Rosa Parks, burning with the injustice of it all, quietly but firmly refused. The bus driver had her arrested and she was sent to trial on 5 December.

Rosa Parks sitting at the front of a bus in Montgomery, Alabama, after segregation was ruled illegal by the Supreme Court.

Parks' arrest caused an uproar. Various groups quickly mobilized, including the Women's Political Council (WPC), which represented African American professional women, and the National Association for the Advancement of Coloured People, a group set up to promote equal rights. At her trial, Parks was found guilty and fined $14 (£5). On the same day, the WPC organized a bus boycott and a group called the Montgomery Improvement Association (MIA) was set up to challenge Montgomery's segregation policy.

Bus boycott

The boycott lasted for 381 days and was widely supported by much of Montgomery's black population. Instead of catching buses they shared taxis or walked to work. The boycott was only lifted after the Supreme Court ruled that segregation was unconstitutional. The ruling may well have been a relief to the bus company, too, as it had suffered financially from losing a large percentage of its passengers.

The civil rights movement (the movement that aimed to abolish discrimination against black Americans) had scored an important victory. One principled woman had stood up to an unfair system and won. It was also a triumph for the MIA, and raised the profile of its leader, a little-known Baptist minister called Martin Luther King, Jr, who would go on to become the most famous leader of the American civil rights movement.

Rosa Parks lost her job as a result of her political battle and was forced to move home in 1957 after receiving death threats. This did not dissuade her from continuing to play an active part in the civil rights movement. In 1987, Parks established the Rosa and Raymond Parks Institute for Self-Development, which encourages young people to further their education and life skills, and learn about the civil rights movement. Rosa Parks died in 2005.

What the papers said

The arrest of a Negro who refused to move to the coloured section of a city bus may bring a court test of segregated transportation in the cradle of the Confederacy. While thousands of other Negroes boycotted Montgomery City Lines in protest, Mrs Rosa Parks was fined $14 in police court yesterday for disregarding a driver's order to move to the rear of a bus last Thursday.

Associated Press, 6 December 1955

eye witness

Oh, she's so sweet. They've messed with the wrong one now!

Unnamed woman in court on seeing Rosa Parks. Quoted on www.time.com/time/time100/heroes/profile/parks03.html

- **FURTHER INFORMATION**
- Books:
  Rosa Parks by Mary Hull
  (Checkmark Books, 2008)
- Websites:
  rosaparks.org
  For information on the work of the Rosa and Raymond Parks Institute

  www.achievement.org/autodoc/page/par0pro-1
  A profile of Rosa Parks and an interview.

The Suez Crisis Begins

The Suez Canal links the Red Sea with the Mediterranean Sea and provides an important access route for ships travelling between Europe and Asia that would otherwise need to sail around Africa. The canal, which cuts through Egyptian territory, was constructed by a French company between 1858 and 1869, and was then owned and operated by mainly British and French shareholders on a 99-year lease from Egypt. The canal proved to be of immense strategic and financial value for the British and French.

Nasser's action

In the early 1950s, as Cold War tensions rose around the world, Egypt decided to ally itself with the Soviet Union rather than with the Western powers, partly because of the West's support for Egypt's enemy, Israel. In retaliation, Britain and the USA withdrew promised funding for Egypt's Aswan Dam project. Egypt's leader, General Gamal Abdel Nasser responded by declaring, on 26 July, that he would nationalize (place under state control) the Suez Canal. He claimed that the revenue raised from the canal would pay for the dam within five years. Nasser's action triggered what became known as the Suez Crisis.

Egyptian Prime Minister Nasser enjoys the adulation of the crowds after announcing the nationalization of the Suez Canal.

Invasion

Britain and France were outraged. They secretly agreed with Israel to invade Egypt, hoping to secure the canal and possibly cause the overthrow of Nasser. The plan was for Israel to invade first. Britain and France would then send in troops and instruct the Israeli and Egyptian armies to withdraw to a distance of 16 kilometres from either side of the canal. An Anglo-

French force would then take control of the area around the canal. On 29 October, Israel invaded Egypt, and two days later Britain and France started a bombing campaign, followed shortly afterwards by an invasion.

The superpowers intervene

This action angered both superpowers. The Soviet Union threatened to join forces with Egypt, and the USA, far from coming to its former allies' aid, was highly critical of the invasion. The American government threatened to sell its reserves of the British pound, thereby causing a collapse of the British currency. The invasion also prompted some Arab countries to impose an oil embargo on Britain and France.

Britain, France and Israel were forced to remove their troops, which were replaced by a United Nations peacekeeping force. The British prime minister, Sir Anthony Eden, resigned as a result of the fiasco. The crisis served as an important lesson for the former world powers, Britain and France, that real power now lay with the USA and Soviet Union.

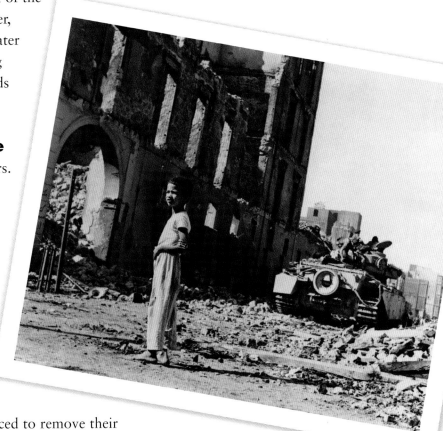

An Egyptian boy stands amid the rubble of ruined buildings in Port Said, Egypt. A British tank can be seen in the background.

What the papers said

Gamal Abdel Nasser's seizure of the Suez Canal can plunge the Middle East into a crisis as deep as any it has known since World War II.

If Egypt gets away with it Nasser may emerge eventually as the master of the Middle East. If he loses this gamble he can wind up on the rubbish heap of former dictators.... If developments should bring about a situation in which the canal were closed, this surely would lead to some kind of military action throwing the entire Arab World into a panic.

Associated Press, 27 July 1956

• **FURTHER INFORMATION**
📖 Books:
The Suez Crisis by Derek Varble (Rosen Publishing Group, 2008)
🖥 Websites:
www.spartacus.schoolnet.co.uk/COLDsuez.htm
Contains interesting source material
http://news.bbc.co.uk/1/hi/world/middle_east/5199392.stm
Suez Crisis: includes maps and photos

The Hungarian Uprising is Crushed

After World War II, Hungary, like the other countries of Eastern Europe, became a communist state, politically and economically dependent on the Soviet Union. Encouraged by the Soviet leadership, the Hungarian government became increasingly repressive, imprisoning and executing thousands of political opponents. After the death of Stalin in 1953 and the 'destalinization' process introduced by his successor Khrushchev, many communist states hoped that Soviet control would decrease.

Students in Budapest defiantly fly the Hungarian flag and brandish weapons during the uprising.

Demonstrations

In Hungary, a series of anti-Soviet demonstrations by students quickly escalated into full-blown riots that threatened to topple the government. On 23 October, the government requested Soviet military assistance. Soviet tanks entered the Hungarian capital Budapest the following day. At the same time, a more popular leader, Imre Nagy, was appointed prime minister. Nagy appealed for calm and offered to introduce political reforms. Soviet troops were withdrawn to garrisons in the Hungarian countryside.

The Soviet Union hoped that this would pacify the protesters. However, Nagy proved far more liberal than they had expected. He released many political prisoners, allowed other political parties to be formed and even formed a coalition government with some of these parties. Then, much to the horror of the Soviet leadership, the Hungarian government discussed leaving the Warsaw Pact (the organization of Eastern European communist states) and, on 1 November, declared itself independent.

The Soviet response

This was a step too far for Khrushchev. A much larger force was sent into Hungary, and on 4 November around 1,000 tanks entered Budapest. Nagy sent a radio broadcast to the West pleading for help, but received no response. The Hungarian army and civilian protesters put up a brave fight, but their resistance was ruthlessly crushed. Within a few days, the fighting was over. Around 3,000 Hungarians were killed, and perhaps 200,000 fled the country. A Soviet-backed government headed by Janos Kadar was installed. In the five years following the uprising, thousands of Hungarians were imprisoned. Nagy himself was arrested and executed in 1958.

The crushing of the Hungarian uprising dealt a severe blow to hopes of democracy in Eastern Europe. Khrushchev had clearly demonstrated that no member country would be permitted to leave the Warsaw Pact. By ignoring Nagy's plea for help, the USA had shown its unwillingness to engage in direct conflict with its superpower rival.

Soviet tanks rumble through Budapest as the uprising is ruthlessly suppressed by the Soviet army.

What the papers said

With no telephonic or telegraphic communications, and with the frontier sealed by Soviet troops on the Hungarian side, no authentic independent news filtered through here today, but it seems only too likely that the (probably improvized) resistance in Budapest was crushed either late yesterday or early this morning.

The Times (London), 6 November 1956

- **SEE ALSO**
  Pages 12–13: 6 March 1953:
  Stalin Dies

- **FURTHER INFORMATION**
  📖 Books:
  Hungary
  by Charlotte Guillain (Raintree, 2012)
  Websites:
  www.spartacus.schoolnet.co.uk/COLD
  hungarianU.htm
  The Hungarian Uprising

Elvis is Censored

When Elvis Presley made his third and final appearance on *The Ed Sullivan Show* in 1957, he was fast becoming one of the biggest stars in the USA. He had already enjoyed a number of hit singles, and his first film, *Love Me Tender*, was doing very well at the box office. However, not everyone approved of the young singer. Many people were worried about some of the movements made by Presley when he was performing. To a modern-day audience he was merely wiggling his hips, but conservative Americans in the 1950s felt these movements were overtly sexual, and therefore indecent. So a remarkable decision was made by the producers of the programme: they would show Elvis from the waist up only.

Television exposure

Presley had graduated from high school in 1953 in Memphis, Tennessee, and started making a name for himself as a singer on the local Country and Western music circuit. In 1955 Presley was taken on by RCA, a major record label, and his records started to attract a national audience. What he needed now was more exposure. That exposure came from *The Ed Sullivan Show*.

The Ed Sullivan Show was one of the most popular programmes on American television. It showcased the talents of all kinds of performers, including composers, singers, magicians, comedians and even performing animals. Importantly, the programme had an eye for what was new and exciting and was the first show to feature rock and roll when Bill Hayley and the Comets played in August 1955. The show appealed to television executives and advertisers because it was popular with all the family, including the new teenage market.

eye witness

This is a real decent fine boy. We've never had a pleasanter experience on our show with a big name than we've had with you. You're thoroughly all right.

Ed Sullivan

A family show

Before Elvis's controversial appearance in 1957, he had already been on *The Ed Sullivan Show* twice before. His first appearance, on 9 September 1956, had attracted a record 60 million viewers, or 80 percent of all those watching television at that particular time.

There had been no complaints following either of his first two

Elvis Presley in characteristic hip-swivelling mode as he performs 'Hillbilly Heartbreak' on stage in Hollywood, California, in June 1956.

performances. Nevertheless, the show's producers were concerned that Presley's performing style might alienate many viewers and harm the programme's reputation as a family show.

The show itself passed without incident. Yet the producer's decision had an unexpected effect. Their crude censorship actually increased the fame of Presley and his hip-swaying antics, and the nickname 'Elvis the Pelvis' firmly stuck. Despite the fact that this was to be Presley's last live television show in the USA, his career was heading straight to the top.

• **SEE ALSO**
Pages 22–23: 30 September 1955: James Dean Dies

• **FURTHER INFORMATION**
Books:
Elvis Presley: Rock & Roll's King
by Stephanie Watson
(Abdo Publishing Company, 2012)
Websites:
www.elvis.com/
The official Elvis Presley website

25

The EEC is Founded

In March 1957, representatives of six European countries met in Rome, Italy, to sign trade and atomic energy agreements. This meeting and the treaties that resulted from it would mark a permanent change in the way Europe worked, traded and viewed itself. The two treaties, known collectively as the Treaty of Rome, were responsible for the formation of the European Economic Community (EEC) and set Europe on the road towards increasing economic and political union.

The six countries that signed the Treaty of Rome were France, Italy, Belgium, Luxembourg, the Netherlands and West Germany. The main aim of the treaty was to bring Europe closer together and improve its prosperity, mostly by changing the way that European countries traded with each other.

Origins

The idea for the EEC was originally suggested by a French politician called Robert Schuman in 1950. Europe had been devastated by two major wars in the first half of the 20th century. Many people in Europe believed that the best way of guaranteeing peace in the future between European nations was through greater economic cooperation. World War II also marked a decisive change in world politics. The USA had emerged as the world's strongest economy and the communist countries had formed their own trading bloc. If the countries of Europe were to compete in the world market, it made sense to work together.

The EEC came into existence on 1 January 1958. The two immediate changes were the formation of the Common Market and a customs union. These abolished all the trade quotas, tariffs and customs barriers that had previously prevented the free movement of people, goods, services and capital between the six countries. The six members also aimed to develop joint policies on labour, social welfare, agriculture, transport and foreign trade, and to work together to oppose anti-competitive practices by large companies.

⊙ eye witness

Make no mistake about it, we are not in business, we are in politics. We are building the United States of Europe.

Walter Hallstein, one of the West German signatories of the Treaty of Rome

Representatives of six European countries sign the Treaty of Rome – actually two treaties that cover the Common Market and the European Atomic Pool.

An economic superpower

The founders of the EEC were idealists. They foresaw a time when Europe would work as one big country, which in turn would make it an economic superpower. Since 1958, there have been subsequent treaties that have altered or amended the Treaty of Rome. One change, in 1993, was to the name of the community; it is now called the European Union (EU). Over the years, many other countries have joined the community, and by January 2007 the EU had 27 member states. It is now the largest single market in the world.

The EU is often divided on many issues, and achieving consensus between member states can be very difficult. In some countries, people see the increasing political power of the EU as a threat to their status as independent nations. Despite this, many countries are keen to join the EU as its power and influence spreads ever wider.

• **FURTHER INFORMATION**
📖 Books:
The European Union
by Peggy Kahn (Chelsea House Publishers, 2012)
🖱 Websites:
europa.eu/
The official site of the European Union

Sputnik is Launched

The Cold War saw no direct armed conflict between the USA and the Soviet Union, but the two superpowers found other arenas in which to compete, and one of these was space. In the 1950s, both countries were keen to be the first to develop technology for the exploration of outer space with artificial satellites and, ultimately, with humans. In October 1957, the Soviet Union scored the first major victory in the space race when it launched a satellite into orbit around the Earth.

Rocket science

During World War II, the Germans had been world leaders in the field of rocket technology, used to create missiles to target enemy territories. After the war, both the USA and the Soviet Union tried to recruit German rocket scientists to help them develop rockets and missiles of their own. It soon became apparent that a rocket had the potential to leave the Earth's atmosphere and enter space. Both the USA and the Soviet Union began developing rockets that could be fired into space, and in 1955 the USA publicly declared its plans to launch a satellite. The fact that the

eye witness

In the open West, you learn to live with the sky. It is a part of your life. But now, somehow, in some new way, the sky seemed almost alien.

Lyndon Baines Johnson, quoted in www.centennialof flight.gov/essay/SPACE FLIGHT/Sputnik/SP16.htm

A Soviet postcard commemorating the launch of the world's first artificial satellites, Sputnik 1 and, on 3 November 1957, Sputnik 2.

Soviet Union managed to do this first was both embarrassing and alarming for the USA.

The Soviets called their satellite Sputnik 1. It was nothing remarkable in itself: just a small, spherical object around 56 centimetres in diameter, which did nothing more than broadcast a simple radio signal as it circled the Earth. The great engineering achievement was the rocket used to place it in orbit.

Sputnik's impact

Sputnik was a concern for the USA and not just because it was now clearly second in the race for space. There was a defence issue here, too: if the Soviet Union could launch a satellite into space, could the Soviets launch missiles directly at American cities? There was also the fear that the Soviets could use future satellites to spy on the USA. It was clear that the American space programme needed more investment. By the end of 1958, the USA had its own space agency, the National Aeronautics and Space Administration, or NASA.

However, the Soviet Union would continue to lead the space race for another decade. Shortly after the launch of Sputnik 1 came Sputnik 2, which carried the first space passenger, a dog called Laika. Then, in 1961, the Soviet Union put the first person into space, an army officer called Yuri Gagarin. It would not be until the moon landing of 1969 that the USA would record a decisive victory in the race to space.

Soviet technicians track the progress of Sputnik as it circles the Earth.

What the papers said

The Soviet Union said its sphere circling the earth had opened the way to interplanetary travel. It did not pass up the opportunity to use the launching for propaganda purposes. It said in its announcement that people now could see how 'the new socialist society' had turned the boldest dreams of mankind into reality.

The New York Times, 5 October 1957

- **SEE ALSO**
  Pages 8–9: 22 January 1952:
  The First Commercial Jet Airliner

- **FURTHER INFORMATION**
  📖 Books:
  Space Race
  by Ton Clohosy Cole (Nobrow Ltd, 2012)
  🔗 Websites:
  http://history.nasa.gov/sputnik
  All about Sputnik on the NASA site

Castro Becomes Prime Minister of Cuba

On New Year's Eve 1958, President Fulgencio Batista of Cuba was forced to flee the country, along with his family and close supporters, as revolutionary forces moved towards the capital, Havana. Batista had himself siezed power in a coup in 1952. As ruler, he ignored Cuba's constitution and banned all political parties. As his rule became increasingly repressive, the Cuban people began to turn against him.

The revolutionary path

Fidel Castro, the man who was to replace Batista as leader, was born in Cuba in 1926. Bright and well educated, Castro studied law at Havana University, and although he began his career as a lawyer he became increasingly involved in politics. However, his political ambitions seemed thwarted when Batista took charge and abolished political parties. Castro became convinced that revolution was the only way to free Cuba from its new dictator.

The 1959 revolution was not the first time Castro had tried to overthrow Batista. In 1953, Castro had led an uprising that had been quickly crushed. His passionate defence during the subsequent trial raised his public profile in Cuba. Castro spent less than two years in prison, and on his release, he moved to Mexico to plan his next campaign.

Fidel Castro (standing in the centre of the photograph) at his secret rebel camp near the coast. This is believed to be the only existing picture of his base. Kneeling in the foreground is Raul Castro, the leader's younger brother.

The 26th of July Movement

Castro returned in 1956 with a small band of fellow revolutionaries. After an early setback, his army, the 26th of July Movement (named after the failed uprising of 1953), slowly began to gain in strength and popular support. They launched guerrilla attacks against government forces and established underground resistance groups in the large towns and cities.

The revolutionaries also won high levels of support among the poor, rural communities. As it became increasingly clear that Batista could not hold on to power, the Cuban army began to switch to Castro's side.

Revolution

The victorious 26th of July Movement rolled into Havana on New Year's Day 1959 amid scenes of triumph and celebration. On 3 January, Castro was named Commander-in-Chief of the Cuban Armed Forces. It was soon evident that the charismatic Castro was attracting much more attention and respect than the new revolutionary government of José Miró Cardona. In February, Miró Cardona unexpectedly resigned and Castro became Prime Minister of Cuba.

Castro went on to become one of the longest-serving national leaders in modern history, leading his country for 47 years until his resignation in July 2006. He followed a socialist agenda, taking Cuban industry into national ownership and expanding public health, welfare and education. His reforms made him popular among many Cubans, but he was also criticized by many others for his intolerance of political dissent, which caused many Cubans to flee from their country.

Almost from the start, Castro's Cuba was hostile to the USA and friendly to the Soviet Union. The presence of a Soviet ally in America's backyard was greatly worrying to the USA, and after 1959, the Cold War grew a little chillier.

A jubilant Fidel Castro waves to the people of Havana in January 1959.

What the papers said

Fidel Castro yielded to the logic of circumstances yesterday and assumed the office of Premier of the Cuban Government. His original idea of letting the Cabinet Ministers [do] their respective jobs while he concentrated on the task of reorganizing the armed forces was clearly unworkable.

The New York Times, February 17 1959

• **FURTHER INFORMATION**
📖 Books:
The Cuban Revolution
by GS Prentzas (Checkmark Books, 2011)
🖥 Websites:
www.npr.org/templates/story/story.php?storyId
=5598311
For a timeline and recordings of Castro's speeches

news.bbc.co.uk/1/hi/world/americas/
country_profiles/1203299.stm
Information on and history of Cuba

Barbie is Launched

In March 1959, the toy manufacturer Mattel unveiled a new product at the American Toy Fair in New York City, USA. It was a plastic doll called Barbie. The doll was 29 centimetres tall and came dressed in a black and white striped swimming costume. What made Barbie different from other dolls was that, rather than being a baby, she was a girl in her late teens. The buyers at the fair were generally unimpressed. No one, including the directors of Mattel, could have predicted what an extraordinary success Barbie would turn out to be.

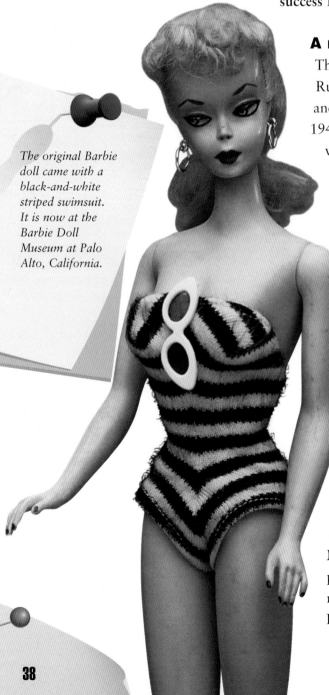

The original Barbie doll came with a black-and-white striped swimsuit. It is now at the Barbie Doll Museum at Palo Alto, California.

A new kind of doll

The Barbie doll was invented by a woman called Ruth Handler who, along with her husband Elliot and friend Harold Matson, had founded Mattel in 1945. Ruth got her inspiration for Barbie from watching her daughter, Barbara, playing with cut-out paper dolls and dressing them in cut-out clothes. Ruth realized that there was no toy equivalent of her daughter's creations – all the dolls on the market were modelled on babies. There were no aspirational dolls out there for little girls to live out their fantasies with. She took the idea to the board of Mattel, but they did not think the idea would work.

Ruth was not to be dissuaded. On a trip to Switzerland she spotted a German doll called Lilli, which was similar to her own idea. Ruth persuaded Mattel to buy the rights for an American version of Lilli and set about improving it. Dressing the doll in different outfits would be a vital part of its appeal, so the clothes had to be good. Ruth hired the fashion designer Charlotte Johnson to design the costumes. The toy had to be affordable, too, so Mattel arranged to manufacture it in China, where production costs were lower. Finally, the doll needed a name, and there was only one possibility: Barbie, the nickname of Ruth's daughter.

Ruth Handler, co-founder of toy manufacturer Mattel, was the driving force behind Barbie.

Billion-seller Barbie

The buyers at the toy fair may have been unmoved, but the general public was extremely keen on the new toy. In the first year, Mattel sold 351,000 dolls at $3 (£1.07) each. Demand was so high that Mattel had difficulty in fulfilling all the orders. That is not to say that everyone was enamoured of the new doll. Some parents worried that it encouraged their daughters to grow up too fast. Later, Barbie's extremely slender build was criticized for promoting an unrealistic body shape for women, which might lead some girls to try to lose weight to look like her. In 1997, Barbie was redesigned with a wider waist.

Despite the occasional controversy, the doll sold, and continues to sell well. The Barbie range has been extended to include a male equivalent, Ken, and several others. Mattel does not give a figure for the number of dolls sold since 1959, but it is thought to run into the billions. The doll launched at the 1959 American Toy Fair has become a superstar.

- **SEE ALSO**
  Pages 20–21: 15 April 1955: The McDonald's Franchise Begins

- **FURTHER INFORMATION**
- Books:
  Inventors and Creators: Ruth Handler: Creator of Barbie by Cynthia Mines (KidHaven Press, 2007)
- Websites:
  http://barbiestyle.barbie.com/history.aspx
  The history of Barbie

03 MAY 1951

The Festival of Britain Opens

The period immediately after World War II was a time of hardship for many people in Britain. Rationing remained in force for food and other consumer goods, and many British cities had yet to be cleared of bomb-damaged buildings. The Labour government decided that the nation needed a boost, and so the Festival of Britain was born.

The Festival of Britain site on the south side of the River Thames.

A tonic for the nation

The aim of the festival was to promote Britain and its achievements in science and the arts. The Labour deputy leader Herbert Morrison described it as 'a tonic for the nation'. It was also seen as a way of advertising the country to the world at large. The festival was timed to coincide with the centenary of the Great Exhibition, a grand display of technological achievements that had been one of the major events of Victorian Britain. The idea of a holding a festival in 1951 was controversial, however. Many people thought that in a time of such hardship, the money would be better spent elsewhere.

Nevertheless, preparations went ahead. An area of land measuring 11 hectares to the south of the River Thames in London was marked out for development as the main festival site. Exhibitions were also planned in other parts of Britain. Building work began in 1948, and, against expectations, was completed in time for the grand opening in May 1951.

● eye witness

I remember that the whole experience was like being on another planet, in a sci-fi way. The modernity of the festival was a wonderland to us all, coming as we did from a very poor background around the bombed sites of the area around the festival grounds.

David Nissen, aged 9. Quoted on www.museumoflondon.org.uk/archive/exhibits/festival/memory_show.asp?disp=true&search=&sfields=all&shownum=10&page=8

The king, George VI, declared the festival open in a live radio broadcast. He and his family then attended a dedication ceremony at the newly built Royal Festival Hall on London's South Bank. The day was marked by a 41-gun salute and cheering, flag-waving crowds.

Futuristic buildings

The main festival site had undergone a major transformation. In place of an abandoned brewery and bombed-out houses, there now stood a complex of strange-looking, futuristic buildings. The buildings were designed in a startlingly modern way, not least the Dome of Discovery, which was at the time the largest dome ever built and the biggest aluminium structure in the world. Another landmark feature was the Skylon, a 76-metre-high, needle-like structure that lit up at night and seemed to hover in mid-air.

The festival was a huge success. Over eight million people visited the main site in the first six months and it actually made a profit. The various other exhibitions and funfairs that were arranged to coincide with the main event were also popular.

However, the festival was not destined to have a longlasting legacy. Once the main site closed in September, most of it was cleared. The futuristic dome and the Skylon were dismantled and sold for scrap. The Royal Festival Hall, however, remained. And London did now have a new centre of culture, the South Bank, which remains very popular to this day. The Festival of Britain certainly acted as a tonic for the nation, and helped to lift people's spirits during a difficult period in the country's history.

The Skylon under construction at the festival site.

- **SEE ALSO**
  Pages 42–43: 2 June 1953: The Coronation of Queen Elizabeth II

- **FURTHER INFORMATION**
  Websites:
  www.museumoflondon.org.uk/archive/exhibits/festival/index.htm
  Comprehensive information and eyewitness accounts

The Coronation of Queen Elizabeth II

On a damp summer's morning in London, three million people lined the streets between Buckingham Palace and Westminster Abbey. They were waiting for a glimpse of Queen Elizabeth II as she made her way to her coronation in a golden carriage known as the State Coach. Elizabeth had been queen since the death of her father King George VI in February 1952. Months of planning, and the hope of fine weather, had delayed the coronation by over a year. Finally, the day had arrived. Ironically, it still rained!

As well as the spectators lining the route, an estimated 11 million listened in on their radios, and over 20 million watched the day's events on television. For many of these viewers, it was the first time they had ever seen a television broadcast. Inside Westminster Abbey, where the coronation was to take place, seating had been arranged to accommodate over 8,000 guests. They included representatives from over 100 different countries, as well as members of the royal family, the aristocracy and the clergy. The abbey also contained an orchestra and 400-voice choir, as well as a sizeable television crew.

The queen steps out of the State Coach on her arrival at Westminster Abbey for the coronation. Her husband, Duke Philip, is to her left.

The ceremony

The queen entered the abbey at 11.20 am, and the ceremony began. She sat in St Edward's Chair, a throne that has been used for coronations since the 1300s. The Archbishop of Canterbury, Geoffrey Fisher, anointed the queen with a special holy oil. She was then given the symbols of sovereignty: the orb, the sceptre of power and justice, the sceptre of mercy, and the royal ring, which signifies the bond between the people and the monarch. Finally, she was crowned with St Edward's Crown, and cries of 'Vivat Regina' ('Long live the Queen') rang out through the abbey.

The queen then moved to the Chair of Homage, and representatives of the aristocracy and clergy pledged their support.

Crowds gather outside Buckingham Palace after the coronation.

The coronation was an interesting mix of ancient and modern. The ceremony itself dated back over 1,000 years, but for the very first time citizens around the country could witness it, thanks to the 20th-century innovation of television.

The coronation lifted the mood of a nation still suffering from hardship and rationing in the aftermath of the recent war. It is estimated that some 93 per cent of the population witnessed the event. It is unlikely that any single event today could hope to attract the same proportion of the population.

- **SEE ALSO**
  Pages 40–41: 3 May 1951:
  The Festival of Britain Opens

- **FURTHER INFORMATION**
  Books:
  Her Story (Queen Elizabeth II) by John Malam (Wayland, 2012)
  Websites:
  www.westminster-abbey.org/our-history/royals/coronations/elizabeth-ii
  Queen Elizabeth II's Coronation

What the papers said

The Archbishop of Canterbury yesterday described the Coronation service as a gathering of Commonwealth nations round the Queen in a tremendous family event, which was really an act of family worship and prayer. With all its magnificence, it was fundamentally simple, and its great dignity was a domestic dignity.

The Times (London), 4 June 1953

The Munich Air Crash

It was a happy Manchester United team that boarded Flight BE609 on its way back home from a European Cup game in Yugoslavia. The team had drawn with Red Star Belgrade and, having already won the home leg, was now through to the next round of the competition. The members of the team had been christened the 'Busby Babes' after their manager, Matt Busby, and because of their youth. In the previous season they had won the English league with an average age of only 22 – the youngest team ever to have done so. They had also reached the semi-finals of the European Cup and were favourites to win it this season.

Engine trouble

The plane needed to stop at Reim Airport in Munich, West Germany, for refuelling before continuing on to Manchester. There was snow on the ground when it landed at Munich. Once the plane had refuelled, the captain, James Thain, attempted to take off. However, halfway down the runway, Thain and his co-pilot decided that the engines did not sound quite right and they abandoned the take-off. The problem, common to this type of plane, was called boost-surging and was the result of a too-rich fuel mixture, causing the engines to misfire. After a short delay, Thain attempted another take-off, but again the pressure gauges showed that the engines were boost-surging, and take-off was abandoned for a second time.

The snow-covered wreckage of the Airspeed Ambassador aircraft at the end of the runway in Munich.

Disaster

In the passenger cabin, the atmosphere had grown quieter. The crew explained that there were some technical problems and there would be a delay while the plane was checked over. It was snowing heavily now and some of the passengers thought the flight might be cancelled. However, at just after 3 pm, the plane was cleared for take-off. This time there was no boost-surging as the plane reached take-off speed.

Then came disaster! Just as the plane was about to leave the ground, its speed fell. The plane crashed through a fence at the end of the runway, then into a house, where it broke up.

At first it was thought the crash had been caused by ice building up on the wings. However, it became apparent that the build-up of slush near the end of the runway was to blame. This caused the plane to lose speed and consequently fail to take off.

A tragic loss

Of the 44 passengers and six crew on the plane that afternoon, 23 died as a result of the crash. Eight Manchester United players – Geoff Bent, Roger Byrne, Eddie Colman, Duncan Edwards, Mark Jones, David Pegg, Tommy Taylor and Billy Whelan – were among the dead, and several more were badly injured, including the manager Matt Busby. The team was all but destroyed. The lives of some of the finest players of their generation had been cut tragically short. It would be a decade before the team would be rebuilt and realize its ambition of lifting the European Cup.

Matt Busby returns home after being released from hospital following the accident.

eye witness

There was a lot of slush flying past the windows and there was a terrible noise, like when a car leaves a smooth road and starts to run over rough ground.

Manchester United player Bill Foulkes, quoted from www.busbybabes.com

• **SEE ALSO**
  Pages 8–9: 22 January 1952:
  The First Commercial Jet Airliner

• **FURTHER INFORMATION**
  📖 Books:
  The Official Illustrated History of Manchester United: The Full Story and Complete Record 1878–2012 (Simon & Schuster Ltd, 2012)
  Websites:
  www.thebusbybabes.com/
  Comprehensive report

People of the Decade

Marlon Brando
(1924–2004)
Marlon Brando was arguably the most exciting movie actor of the 1950s. He was one of the greatest early exponents of the technique known as method acting, in which the actor attempts to identify with the emotions of the character being played. Brando gave electrifying performances in films such as *A Streetcar Named Desire* (1951), *The Wild One* (1953) and *On the Waterfront* (1954) for which he won an Oscar. He was an inspiration for many young actors, including James Dean and Jack Nicholson, and his influence continues to this day.

Sir Winston Churchill
(1874–1965)
Britain's charismatic war leader returned as prime minister in 1951 and continued in office until his resignation in 1955. He was also a prolific painter and author, receiving the Nobel Prize for Literature in 1953. In that year he was also knighted by the newly crowned Queen Elizabeth II. Churchill was an early supporter of closer ties with Europe, but also sought to maintain a special relationship with the USA.

Albert Einstein
(1879–1955)
The year 1955 witnessed the death of one of the world's greatest scientists. So famous was he that most ordinary people had not only heard of him but would recognize a picture of him, too. In 1905, Einstein proposed his special theory of relativity, followed ten years later by his general theory of relativity. These two towering achievements transformed for ever the way physicists looked at the universe. He received the Nobel Prize in Physics for his work in 1921.

Dwight D Eisenhower
(1890–1969)
Eisenhower was the 34th president of the USA. During World War II he had been Supreme Commander of the Allied Troops invading France and was later the Supreme Commander of the newly-formed NATO. He was elected president in the Republican Party's comprehensive election victory of 1952 and remained in office until 1961.

Charles de Gaulle
(1890–1970)
In 1958, Charles de Gaulle, wartime leader of the Free French and first post-war leader of France, became prime minister again, following the political turmoil that resulted from the uprising in the French colony of Algiers. While in office, de Gaulle drafted a new constitution, which the French people voted to accept, and he was made president in 1959.

Pope John XXIII
(1881–1963)
Following the death of Pope Pius XII in 1958, Cardinal Angelo Roncalli was elected pope and became the leader of the Roman Catholic Church. Taking the name John XXIII, he began his papacy by visiting hospitals and prisons – unheard-of behaviour for a pope. This, along with his gentle and smiling demeanour, made him extremely popular. He would go on to introduce major reforms to the Catholic Church, bringing the congregation into closer participation with church services and improving relations with other religions.

Harold Macmillan
(1894–1986)
Harold Macmillan was an effective member of the Conservative administration of the 1950s, occupying a number of cabinet positions before taking over as prime minister in 1956 when Anthony Eden stepped down after the Suez Crisis. Macmillan was initially a lucky Prime Minister. The British economy was improving and people generally felt better about life. He won the general election of 1959 and was popular enough to earn the nickname Supermac. He resigned in 1963 due to ill health, possibly made worse by a scandal that severely damaged his government.

J R R Tolkien
(1892–1973)
John Ronald Reuel Tolkien was a professor of Anglo-Saxon at Oxford University and a prolific writer. His most famous work, *The Lord of the Rings*, was published in three volumes between 1954 and 1955. It began as a sequel to his earlier work, *The Hobbit*, but became a much larger story. *The Lord of the Rings* is a fantasy epic peopled with creatures such as hobbits, elves, dwarves and orcs, as well as humans. It has become one of the most popular books in 20th-century literature.

Harry S Truman
(1884–1972)
Harry S Truman became the 33rd president of the USA in 1945, following the death in office of his predecessor Franklin D Roosevelt. Truman took over just as World War II was ending and the Cold War was starting to loom. In 1950, Truman intervened as North Korea invaded South Korea. He sent in troops in support of South Korea. Meanwhile, at home, Truman's administration came under attack as Joseph McCarthy began his anti-communist witch hunts, claiming the government itself was harbouring enemies of the state. He lost the 1952 presidential election to Dwight D Eisenhower.

Glossary

administration The government of a country.

aspirational Describing an object that inspires a person towards self-improvement.

Bolshevik A communist political party in Russia.

ceasefire An agreement between opposing sides in a conflict that they will stop fighting, usually to enable peace talks to take place.

Central Committee In the Soviet Union the part of the government that was responsible for party policy.

cinder race track During the 1950s athletic tracks were constructed from cinder which came from cooled lava and provided grip on the running surface.

civil rights The rights that all citizens of a society are supposed to enjoy, such as the right to vote or the right to receive fair treatment from the law.

commercial air travel The use of air transport by ordinary civilians or commercial companies, as distinct from military air transport.

communist A believer in state control of the economy and the equal distribution of wealth.

destalinization The move away from Stalin's policies, and the introduction of a less ruthless style of government, by the leaders of the Soviet Union.

discrimination The unfair treatment of a person or group, usually because of prejudice about, for example, their race, ethnic group, religion or sexuality.

European Cup A football tournament in which the champions of national football leagues across Europe competed against each other in a knock-out competition. It has since been replaced by the Champions League.

ideology A system of beliefs and ideas that form the basis for a political philosophy or programme.

franchise An agreement to sell a company's products exclusively in a particular area or to operate a business that carries that company's name.

fuel mixture The mixture of fuel and air required to make combustion engines work. A 'too-rich' fuel mixture contains too much fuel in relation to the amount of air in the mixture.

guerrilla A member of an independent fighting force usually with some political aim such as the overthrow of a government.

Marx, Karl A German political philosopher (1818–1883) whose ideas inspired, among others, communist revolutionaries in Russia and, later, China.

NATO The North Atlantic Treaty Organisation is a military alliance established in 1949 by the USA and a number of Western European countries to promote collective security during the Cold War.

organ transplant The transfer of an organ (such as a heart, kidney or lung) from one person to another.

rationing A restriction on what foodstuffs and goods a person may purchase, usually in times of shortages such as during a war.

Republican Party One of the two main political parties in the USA. The other main party is the Democratic Party.

revolution The overthrow of a government or political system.

revolutionary A person who takes an active role in a revolution.

Roman Catholic Church A Christian Church that has a pope as its head and is administered from the Vatican City in Rome.

satellite A device that is sent into space and moves around the earth. It is used for communication.

Secretary of State The US government official who is in charge of foreign policy.

sovereignty The authority to rule over a state.

Soviet Union Also known as the USSR (Union of Soviet Socialist Republics), a country formed from the territories of the Russian Empire in 1917, which lasted until 1991.

socialist Relating to, or belief in, a political system in which wealth is shared equally between people, and the main industries and trade are controlled by the government.

space race The Cold War-inspired competition between the USA and the Soviet Union, which lasted roughly from 1957 to 1975, to be the first to explore outer space with artificial satellites and, later, with humans.

superpowers An extremely powerful nation with greater political, economic or military power than most other nations. The term was used to describe the USA and the Soviet Union during the Cold War period.

unconstitutional Against the principles set out in a country's constitution. A constitution is a written statement containing the basic laws or principles by which a country is governed.

USSR *see* Soviet Union

United Nations An organization of nations, formed in 1945, to promote peace, security and international cooperation.

witch-hunt A systematic campaign directed against people who hold different views. The term refers back to the time when women were put to death in the belief that they were witches.

Index

Page numbers in **bold** refer to illustrations